P9-ELW-715

A Note to Parents and Teachers

Kids can imagine, kids can laugh and kids can learn to read with this exciting new series of first readers. Each book in the Kids Can Read series has been especially written, illustrated and designed for beginning readers. Humorous, easy-to-read stories, appealing characters and topics, and engaging illustrations make for books that kids will want to read over and over again.

To make selecting a book easy for kids, parents and teachers, the Kids Can Read series offers three levels based on different reading abilities:

Level 1: Kids Can Start to Read

Short stories, simple sentences, easy vocabulary, lots of repetition and visual clues for kids just beginning to read.

Level 2: Kids Can Read with Help

Longer stories, varied sentences, increased vocabulary, some repetition and visual clues for kids who have some reading skills, but may need a little help.

Level 3: Kids Can Read Alone

More challenging topics, more complex sentences, advanced vocabulary, language play, minimal repetition and visual clues for kids who are reading by themselves.

With the Kids Can Read series, kids can enter a new and exciting world of reading!

Marie Curie

With much love to Julia, another creative
and very brave Polish woman — E.M.

To Samantha — J.M.

The publisher and author wish to express their gratitude and appreciation to
Dr. Allan Griffin, Department of Physics, University of Toronto, for his review of
the text. While every effort has been made to ensure accuracy, any errors are the
responsibility of the author and publisher.

Kids Can Read ® Kids Can Read is a registered trademark of Kids Can Press Ltd.

Kids Can Press acknowledges the financial support of the Government of
Ontario, through the Ontario Media Development Corporation's Ontario Book
Initiative; the Ontario Arts Council; the Canada Council for the Arts; and the
Government of Canada, through the BPIDP, for our publishing activity.

Published in Canada by
Kids Can Press Ltd.
29 Birch Avenue
Toronto, ON M4V 1E2

Published in the U.S. by
Kids Can Press Ltd.
2250 Military Road
Tonawanda, NY 14150

www.kidscanpress.com

Edited by David MacDonald
Designed by Marie Bartholomew
Printed and bound in Singapore

The paper used to print this book was produced with elemental chlorine-free
pulp harvested from managed sustainable forests.

The hardcover edition of this book is smyth sewn casebound.
The paperback edition of this book is limp sewn with a drawn-on cover.

CM 09 0 9 8 7 6 5 4 3 2 1   CM PA 09 0 9 8 7 6 5 4 3 2 1

Library and Archives Canada Cataloguing in Publication

MacLeod, Elizabeth
     Marie Curie / written by Elizabeth MacLeod ;
illustrated by John Mantha.

(Kids Can read)
ISBN 978-1-55453-296-4 (bound).
ISBN 978-1-55453-297-1 (pbk.)

1. Curie, Marie, 1867–1934—Juvenile literature. 2. Women chemists—Poland—
Biography—Juvenile literature. 3. Women physicists—Poland—Biography—
Juvenile literature. I. Mantha, John II. Title. III. Series: Kids Can read
(Toronto, Ont.)

QD22.C8M32 2009   j540.92   C2008-904470-3

Kids Can Press is a *corus*™ Entertainment company

Marie Curie

Written by Elizabeth MacLeod
Illustrated by John Mantha

Kids Can Press

One of the most famous scientists ever! The first woman to win the world's top science prize! The first person to win it twice!

Marie Curie was all of these things.

Marie was always very shy. Winning awards did not mean much to her. Making discoveries in her lab was more important to Marie.

Marya

Marie grew up in Poland, in the city of
Warsaw. When she was young, she was
called Marya (MAR-ee-ah).

Marya was the youngest in her family.
She had three sisters and one brother.

Marya loved school — most of the time. She was very smart and she found it easy to memorize.

Marya was often asked to say poems from memory for visitors. Marya hated this because she was so shy.

Marya finished high school with the best marks in her class. But she had worked so hard that she became sick. Her father sent her to visit relatives in the country.

There, Marya had lots of fun. At one party, she danced so much that she wore through a new pair of shoes!

After a year, Marya returned to Warsaw.
What would she do now? In Poland,
women were not allowed to go to university.
Marya could go to school in another country,
but that would cost a lot of money.

Marya decided to get a job. She hoped to earn enough money to go to university in Paris, France.

A rich family hired Marya as a teacher. Soon, she fell in love with the family's oldest son. But his parents would not let him marry a teacher with little money.

Marya's heart was broken. But she kept working for the family. She needed the money.

By 1891, Marya finally had made enough money to go to school in Paris.

In Paris, Marya was called Marie. She studied science at university.

Marie had to work hard. She did not speak French well. But Marie often got the best marks in her class.

To save money, Marie lived in the cheapest place she could find. During the winter, her room was freezing cold.

One night, Marie was shivering in bed. To get warm, she piled all her clothes on top of the bed!

Marie finished university at the top of her class. While she was looking for a lab to work in, Marie met Pierre Curie.

Pierre was a very famous scientist. He quickly fell in love with Marie. Many men give flowers to women they like. Not Pierre — he gave Marie one of his science reports!

Pierre soon asked Marie to marry him. She worried that she would never return to Poland if she married Pierre. But she loved him.

In 1895, Marie and Pierre were married. Two years later, their daughter Irène (ee-REN) was born.

Marie began studying rocks that
contained a metal called uranium. She had
heard that uranium gives off invisible rays.
Scientists call these rays "radiation." Marie
wanted to learn more about radiation.

Pierre worked with Marie. They realized the rocks must contain metals other than uranium that also gave off radiation.

Marie and Pierre were excited. Did their rocks contain metals that scientists did not know about? They had to find out.

In 1898, Marie found a new metal in the rocks. She called it "polonium" because the name sounds like "Poland."

Were there other new metals in the rocks, waiting to be discovered?

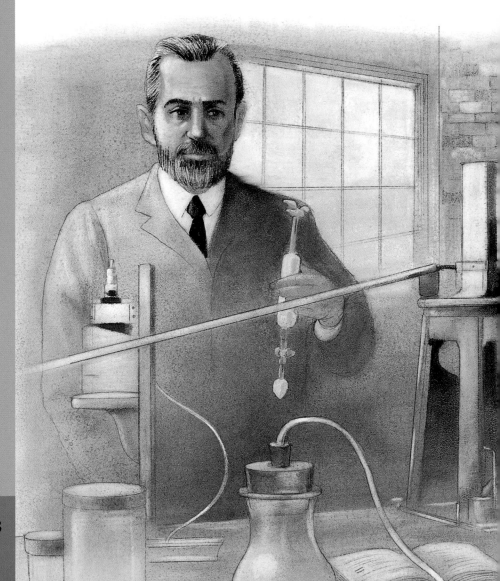

Marie soon discovered another new metal. She named it "radium" because this name sounds like the word "radiation."

Now Marie and Pierre had to prove that radium and polonium really were new. To do that, they had to produce small chunks of each metal. Each chunk had to contain no other metal.

Marie chose to work first on radium.

Marie and Pierre had little money. Marie had to work in a cold, leaky shed. There, she melted and stirred rocks in huge pots.

Four years later, in 1902, Marie produced a chunk that contained only radium. She really had discovered a new metal!

In 1903, Marie and Pierre won a Nobel
Prize. This is the world's most famous
science award. The Curies won it for their
work with radiation.

Marie was the first Polish person, and
the first woman, to win this prize.

Pierre became a professor at the university in Paris. Marie was in charge of his lab. Finally she had a warm lab where she could work!

Even better, the Curies had a second daughter, Eve, in 1904.

On a rainy day in 1906, Pierre was hurrying to a meeting. Suddenly he slipped, right in front of horses pulling a wagon!

The wagon ran over him. Pierre was killed.

Marie was very sad. She missed Pierre so much.

The university where Pierre had taught gave Marie his job. She became the first woman to teach there.

Huge crowds came to Marie's first class. They wondered if she might cry about Pierre. Instead, Marie quietly started teaching just where Pierre had stopped.

In 1911, Marie won another Nobel Prize for her work.

In 1914, many countries began fighting a war. Soon, France was attacked.

Marie knew about an invention called the X-ray machine. This machine would be useful in the war. It would let doctors see bullets and broken bones in soldiers.

Marie, her daughter Irène and many others drove X-ray machines to the battlefields. There, they used the machines to help soldiers who had been hurt.

It was dangerous work, but Marie and her helpers were very brave.

Marie was happy when the war ended in 1918. Both France and Poland were on the winning side.

Soon, scientists realized how dangerous radiation could be. It was too late for Marie. She was going blind, probably because of her experiments with radium and polonium.

Marie kept working. Her daughter Irène
and Irène's husband, Frédéric, joined her.

In 1934, Marie died from a blood disease
that was caused by radiation.

Marie had worried that people would use her discoveries to make weapons. Sadly, she was right. Scientists soon used uranium to make powerful bombs.

But scientists have found many other uses for radiation. They use it to help people with cancer. It can even help scientists figure out the age of dinosaur bones!

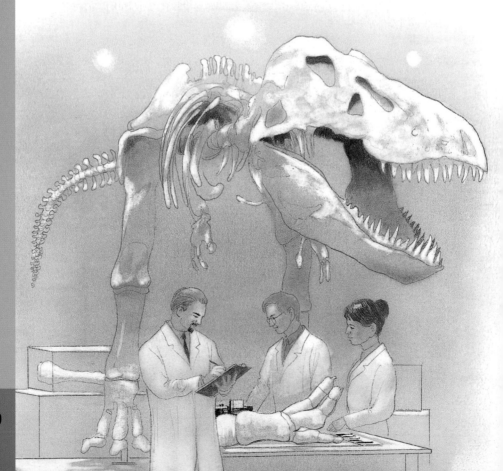

Radiation can be used to make electricity. Experts also use radiation to find weak spots in bridges.

Marie led the way for girls and women to study science. Today, she is still the most famous woman scientist.

More facts about Marie

• Marie was born on November 7, 1867. She died on July 4, 1934.

• Marie created the word "radioactive" for metals that give off radiation.

• Marie and Irène are the only mother and daughter who both have won Nobel Prizes.

Look for these other Level 3 books in the Kids Can Read series

Visit www.kidscanpress.com for more information